Gather Yourself

My Early Journey through Grief

Shannon Leigh

ISBN 978-1-63630-002-3 (Paperback)
ISBN 978-1-63630-003-0 (Digital)

Covenant Books, Inc.
11661 Hwy 707
Murrells Inlet, SC 29576
www.covenantbooks.com

Contents

There are times in our lives when we must gather ourselves. All of our "self." Gather…our sad self, our happy self, our serious self, our silly self, our hyper self, our chill self, our angry self, our cheerful self, our begrudging self, our forgiving self, our bitter self, our loving self, our generous self, our selfish self, our broken self, our redeemed self, our grateful self, our rude self, our peaceful self, our irritated self, our content self, our annoyed self, our joyful self, our resentful self, our turbulent self, our calm self, our fuming self, our collected self. We must gather it all. We have to feel it to heal it. Keep moving forward. Then, gather your people. Your family, friends, and loved ones. Your tribe. Your squad. Your posse. Your crew. Gather yourself, then gather your people.

So…sometimes we can get off track. Off of our path. Off of the trail. Maybe we were distracted. Something else had our attention that really shouldn't have had our attention. Maybe something shiny blinded us. We couldn't see and we took the wrong fork in the road. Or maybe it's our own fault. We were selfish and we made the wrong choices. So now what? What to do? First of all, we have to realize that we are on the wrong path. Something has to get our attention. Namely, the Holy Spirit has to nudge us, wake us, and speak to us that we are off track. That means…we have to be open to hearing from and sensing the Holy Spirit. Then…we must keep our eyes, hearts, and minds focused on getting back on the right path—our intended path. We keep pressing forward until we find someone that can help us, give us directions, and guide us back to our trail.

Today, I noticed this tree.
Large.
Big, full healthy.
Strong.
Pretty.
Then I noticed that it had cracked during a storm.
The trunk was hollow.
Empty.
The tree had been dead inside.
That's how we are without salvation thru Jesus.
Dead and rotting inside.
Empty.
We may look good on the outside.
But sick with sin on the inside.
Rotting and dying.

During my mom's illness, our church family and friends brought food. So much food, and we were so very thankful for each one of them. After mom's passing, the food kept coming for quite some time. Then as we had holidays and special family events, I realized there are so many dishes and recipes that reminded me of my mom. There were so many casseroles and desserts that she made and I knew she would never make them for us again. Then I thought, that's what we do in our culture but also as a human race, we bring food during difficult times. We bring food for grieving friends and family. So I realized, we work through our grief and during the process of gathering 'yourself', we gather together to share meals. There can be a lot of love in a casserole. I wanted to include some special dishes here that remind me of my mom and some dishes that are special to me. Some of these have lots of memories, a lifetime of memories for me, and some of them are special for just one reason. Anyway, when you make these recipes, I hope you feel lots of love, as my mom made these with love or they were made for her with lots of love.

"Breakfast" My Mom's Least Favorite Meal

Sausage Casserole

Cook 1 pound sausage and drain. Mix with 1 block of cream cheese. Layer crescent roll dough in bottom of 6x10 dish. Place sausage mixture in dish. Cover with second tube of rolls. Follow directions for baking the rolls.

For a 9x13 pan, use 2 pounds sausage, 2 cream cheese blocks, and 4 crescent roll tubes.

Diesel Waffles

2 cups flour
2 tablespoons baking powder
3/4 teaspoon salt
3 egg yolks beaten
1 3/4 cups of milk
1/3 cup of vegetable oil

Mix and spoon into waffle iron.

Spinach Bacon Quiche

1 lb. bacon, cooked and crumbled
1 (9 inch) deep dish refrigerated pie crust
6 large eggs beaten
1 1/2 cups heavy cream
salt and pepper to taste
2 cups chopped fresh spinach
2 dashes Worcestershire sauce
5 dashes of hot sauce or to taste
1 1/2 cups of shredded cheddar cheese

Preheat oven to 375 degrees. Whisk together eggs, cream, salt and pepper, hot sauce, and Worcestershire sauce. Spread spinach on the bottom of the pie crust, then cover with bacon crumbles and cheddar cheese. Pour the egg mixture on top.

Bake in preheated oven until the top is lightly brown and puffed, and a knife inserted into the center of the quiche comes out clean, approximately 35 to 45 minutes (I typically have to bake mine for an additional 20 minutes).

Sausage Balls

3 cups Bisquick
1 lb. sausage
12 oz. cheddar cheese, shredded

Melt cheese. Mix other ingredients together. Roll into 1 inch balls. Bake on cookie sheet at 350 degrees for 20 minutes.

Appetizers/Sides/Salads

Five Cup Salad

1 cup pineapple chunks (drained)
1 cup mandarin oranges (drained)
1 cup coconut
1 cup mini marshmallows
1 cup sour cream

Mix and refrigerate

Jordan's Slaw

Jordan was my mom's kidney donor on September 3, 2015. As a family, we established a close relationship with Jordan's family after we were all able to meet each other. Jordan's mom shared this favorite recipe of his with my mom. My mom made this slaw quite often, as she actually had cravings for it.

2 (12 oz.) bags of broccoli coleslaw
2 (3 oz.) bags ramen noodle soup packets (chicken flavor) but you
    can use any flavor
3/4 cup stick butter
1/4 cup slivered almonds
1/4 cup sunflower seeds
chopped green onions for garnish

Dressing Mix
3/4 cup canola oil
1/4 cup brown or white sugar
1/4 cup apple cider vinegar
1 ramen noodle seasoning packet

Place noodles in a bag and crush them while melting the butter in a saucepan over low heat. Add the crushed noodles and slivered almonds to the skillet and sauté until golden brown. Meanwhile, whisk together all the dressing ingredients in a bowl. Place the shredded broccoli into a bowl and toss with the noodles, almonds, and sunflower seeds. Pour the dressing over the salad and toss to coat. Garnish with green onions.

Spinach Dip

1 pkg. frozen chopped spinach, thawed and drained.
1 16 oz. container sour cream
1 cup Hellman's mayonnaise
1 pkg. Knorr vegetable soup, dip, and recipe mix
1 8 oz. can water chestnuts, drained and chopped
3 green onions, chopped

Stir together spinach, sour cream, mayonnaise, soup mix, water chestnuts, and green onions.

Cover and chill for two hours to blend flavors.

Stir well before serving. You can serve with vegetables or tortilla chips. We always loved this dip with Kings Hawaiian rolls cut into cubes.

Football Game Day Bean Dip

2 cans jalapeno bean dip
1 lb. ground beef
1 16 oz. jar picante sauce
1 8 oz. carton sour cream
8 oz. shredded cheddar cheese
1 bunch green onions

Spread bean dip into bottom of large baking dish. Top with browned and drained ground beef. Add chopped onions and half of the picante sauce. Sprinkle with cheese and sour cream then add the remaining picante sauce. Bake at 450 until hot and bubbly. May garnish with black olives, salsa, and guacamole. Serve hot with tortilla chips.

Waldorf Salad

2 cups diced apples (red and green)
2 tbsps. lemon juice
1 cup chopped celery
1/2 cup seedless raisins, plumped in warm water
1 cup mini marshmallows
1/4 cup mayonnaise
1/4 cup heavy cream, whipped
optional—1/2 cup broken walnuts or pecans

Dip apple pieces in lemon juice to preserve freshness and color. Then drain. Allow raisins to soak in hot water until plumped and full, then drain. Stir together apples, celery, raisins, marshmallows, and mayonnaise in a large mixing bowl. Fold in the whipped cream and the nuts. (We typically double this recipe because we can never get enough.)

Freezer Slaw

1 medium head of cabbage, chopped
2 carrots peeled and shredded
1 sweet pepper
1 tsp. salt
1 1/2 cups sugar
1 cup white vinegar
1/4 cup water
1 tsp. mustard seed
1 tsp. celery seed

Mix cabbage, carrots, salt, and sweet pepper. Let stand for 1 hour and squeeze out any excess juice. While the cabbage is sitting, mix together the remaining ingredients to make a syrup. Boil for about 1 minute and let stand until lukewarm. Pour over the cabbage mix. Place into containers and freeze. We like to thaw this out later and top with some French dressing.

Main Dishes

Sweet Sue's Squash Casserole

8 cups squash and zucchini cut into chunks
1/2 lb. mild sausage, cooked and drained
1 cup onion sautéed

Mix together and place in baking dish.

1 can cream of mushroom soup
2 cups milk
1/2 cup Bisquick
salt and pepper to taste

Mix and place over the squash and sausage mixture.

Top with 1 cup shredded cheese, 1/2 sleeve Ritz crackers crushed and 1 cup of herb seasoned stuffing
cover with 1/2 stick of melted butter.
Bake 350 degrees for 30 minutes uncovered and then 30 minutes covered.
This was the last food that my mom could really taste and enjoy.

Chicken and Cheese Quesadilla

2 boneless, skinless chicken breast halves chopped
1 can Rotel Mexican Festival
4 (10-inch) flour tortillas
1 cup each: shredded Monterey Jack and Cheddar cheese blended

In a large skillet cook chicken with Rotel (about 10 minutes) until the chicken is no longer pink and the liquid has reduced. Set aside. Place tortillas on a flat work surface. Spread 1/4 of the chicken mixture over half of each tortilla, within 1 inch of each edge. Top chicken mixture with 1/2 cup cheese blend. Fold tortilla to close. Heat a second skillet over medium heat. Cook quesadillas until slightly crisp, about 5 minutes per side. Cut each quesadilla into wedges.

This was the last food mom requested that I made for her. She ate a few bites. But said they were really good.

New Year's Day Soup

1 1/2 cups dried black eyed peas
4 tablespoons of bacon grease drippings (bacon fat)
1 cup chopped onion
4 celery ribs chopped
3 carrots peeled and chopped
4 garlic cloves, minced
1 1/2 teaspoons dried thyme, divided
8 cups chicken or beef stock
1 ham hock or some chopped bone-in ham
salt and pepper to taste

Sort peas and soak on water overnight. Melt bacon grease in skillet, add onion, celery, carrots, and garlic. Cook over low heat until vegetables are tender. Stir in 1 teaspoon of thyme and stock. Add ham and peas (drained). Bring to boil. Add salt and pepper. Reduce heat and simmer until peas are tender (about 40 minutes). Skim occasionally. Add remaining thyme if desired.

Mom made this every New Year's Day.

Ma's Arizona Corn

1 pkg. Mahatma yellow rice cooked according to package directions.
1 can Mexican Corn
1 can cream of celery soup
1–2 cups mild cheddar cheese, shredded

Mix rice, corn, and soup and place in 8x8 baking dish. Cover with cheese. Bake 350 degrees until bubbly.

West Spanish Rice

1 lb. ground beef
1 large onion chopped
1 can tomato sauce
2 cans Veg-All
1 cup Minute Rice

Brown the ground beef, drain, then add onion and simmer. Add tomato sauce, Veg-All, and rice. Let simmer until rice is done. Don't overcook or the rice will get mushy.

Mine and Yours Spaghetti Sauce

3 pounds ground beef browned
1 large celery rib chopped
1 large onion chopped
1/2 of a large green pepper chopped
2 cans stewed tomatoes
1 can tomato sauce
6 shakes of garlic powder
salt and pepper to taste

Combine all in crock pot and let slow cook all day.

Chicken Noodle Soup to Make You Feel Better

1 medium bag of baby carrots chopped
1 bunch of celery chopped
2 12 oz. cans of chicken breast or 3 cups of cooked chicken pulled
    off the bone
1 bag egg noodles
8–10 chicken bouillon cubes

Boil egg noodles and set aside.

Boil 2 cups water with 2 bouillon cubes, then place celery and carrots. Add remaining cubes and 1 cup of water per bouillon cube added. Add chicken. Boil until cubes are completely dissolved. Then add cooked noodles. Boil together for a couple of minutes and remove from heat.

Mom's Sage Dressing

1 large iron skillet of cooked cornbread
6 slices of white loaf bread
2 cups (1 can) chicken broth
1/2 cup of milk
1 cup of celery chopped
1 cup of onion chopped
1/4 cup of butter
2–3 teaspoons of sage
a pinch of thyme
1 egg beaten
salt and pepper to taste

Crumble all bread in large bowl. Pour broth and milk over crumbs. Sauté celery and onions in butter until tender. Add to bread mixture. Stir in remaining ingredients. Then place mixture in 9x12 aluminum baking pan. Cover and bake at 400 degrees for 15 minutes or until heated through.

Desserts

Lemon Bars

1 cup sweetened condensed milk
1/2 cup lemon juice
1 1/2 cups flour
1 cup oats
1 cup brown sugar
2/3 cup butter melted

Combine first two ingredients and set aside.

Combine remaining ingredients. Press the oat mixture into the bottom of a 9x13 inch pan (saving about 1/2 cup for topping). Pour the lemon juice mixture over the top. Then sprinkle remaining oat crumbles on top of lemon juice mixture. Bake at 350 degrees for 35 minutes. Cool. Cut into squares and refrigerate.

Mom said these were healthy because they had oats in them.

Grandma Vada's Birthday Cake with Chocolate Cooked Icing—Daddy's Favorite

2 cups sifted flour
1 1/4 cups sugar
1/2 cup Crisco shortening
1 1/2 cups milk
3 eggs
1 tsp. vanilla

Combine flour, sugar, shortening, and slightly more than half of the milk. Blend together. Beat for 2 minutes. Add remaining milk, eggs, vanilla. Beat 2 minutes. Bake in preheated oven at 350 degrees for 25 to 30 minutes.

Icing:
2 cups sugar
2 tablespoons (heaping) cocoa
1 cup of milk

Cook over low/medium heat until a hard ball forms in cold water (much like cooking fudge). Stir a little and add 1 teaspoon of vanilla and 1/3 stick of butter.

Mix a bit more. Let cool a little. Spread on cake before hardening.

Apricot Salad

2 small packages apricot gelatin
2 cups hot water
2 cups cold water
1 cup crushed pineapple (save juice)
1 cup of small marshmallows
2 sliced bananas

Mix gelatin and hot water until dissolved. Add cold water, drained crushed pineapple, and banana slices. Place in 9x13 glass dish. Place the marshmallows on top.

For topping, combine 1/2 cup sugar, 1/2 cup of reserved pineapple juice, 2 tablespoons of butter. Cook over low heat until sugar dissolves. Then add 2 tablespoons of flour. When smooth, add 1 egg (beaten), and cook until thick. Add 1 block of cream cheese while still warm. Mix. When cream cheese melts, pour gently over gelatin mixture on top of marshmallows. Refrigerate. Serve when gelatin is set.

SJ's Best Pumpkin Cake

2 cups flour
2 cups sugar
2 tsps. cinnamon
1 cup of oil
4 eggs
2 cups pumpkin

Mix together.

Grease and flour a bundt pan. Bake at 350 for 45 minutes in fully preheated oven. Let cool 5 minutes and invert on cake plate.

Cream Cheese Icing:
1 stick butter
1 tsp. vanilla
1 cup chopped pecans
8 oz. cream cheese
1 box confectioners' sugar

Mix and place on cooled pumpkin cake.

Vada's Sugar Cookies and Ma's Valentine Cookies

1 cup sugar
1/2 cup shortening
1 egg
3 cups flour
1/2 tsp vanilla
1/2 cup milk

Cream the shortening and sugar. Add egg and beat well. Add flour, milk, and vanilla. Mix thoroughly. Roll on floured surface to 1/2 inch thickness. Cut into desired shaped. Bake at 350 for 10 to 15 minutes. Makes approximately 3 dozen cookies. Ice with powdered sugar and butter icing.

The day of my mom's biopsy, she, my daddy, and I, sat in the hospital room together waiting until the time for the procedure arrived. It stormed *all day long*. Heavy rain, strong wind, and lightning. We watched through the large window in the room as the storm hung over us. My mom went for her biopsy in the late afternoon. I sat with daddy and fielded calls from surgery staff and the surgeon himself.

When the bad results were delivered, I had to tell my daddy. "Yes, the results are the worst news we could hear. It's bad." I stayed until mom got back to the room and I ordered her some dinner (Jell-O, juice, and broth). I helped her with bathroom duties and got her mostly tucked into bed. I left for home hoping the rain would ease up a bit.

As I drove toward home in complete silence on I-40 East, the rain had slowed. After driving for about an hour, something in my rear view mirror caught my eye. The sun had broken through the storm clouds and was beginning to set in its spot in the western sky. My very first thought was, *Oh thank you, God! The sun is shining on my Momma! Everything's going to be okay.*

Then God spoke to me. He said, "The sun is setting on your mom."

At first I wanted to argue with him, "No, God, the sun is out now and the storm is gone. It's all going to be okay."

God replied, "Shannon, the sun is setting on your mom's life."

I get *so* tired from being on the 'verge of tears.'

Constantly. Any period of quiet exponentiates 'the verge.' What is the verge of tears anyway? It means close to, near to, on the brink or border of something. So, basically, I'm about to cry or my eyes are about to leak, sixteen to eighteen hours of every single day. When will this go away? Sometimes I can let my eyes leak and feel all the emotions. Other times, it's just not the appropriate place or time. Sometimes I wonder if I just let myself feel all the feelings at the time that I'm feeling them, if maybe all the feelings would stop coming at me all the time. If I just let them all out, free them, then maybe I wouldn't be constantly 'on the verge.' I still haven't decided what I'm going to do.

Mom told me today that she wanted to stop treatment and she wanted to be kept comfortable. The following thirty minutes that we talked alone, prayed, and prayed together was one of the most special times of my entire life. It was heartbreaking, gut-wrenching, and beautiful. She cried, telling me how much she loved me. We laughed at funny memories. I recalled *so* many times in my life when she bailed me out, helped me through, and why I thought she was the best mom ever.

I text Travis and he came up to the house and we talked. Then, I got daddy and brought him out to the back porch and we told him. He was actually relieved. Daddy had been caring for mom every single day, all day long as she very steadily became sicker and weaker each and every day, to the point that she could no longer walk or bear her own body weight. While Travis and I sat there talking with daddy, it began to rain and then the rain started to pour. There's no doubt in my mind that God was raining down tears from heaven, crying with us in our sorrow. But God will comfort us and keep us. He will bring us thru this.

When I left Mom and Dad's, the sun was shining. ☀

You know when I helped daddy go thru Mom's clothes I wasn't really emotionally ready to do it, but he was, so I did. Later on, like a couple of weeks later, I was looking through the things that I kept of hers and I couldn't find her bathrobe. I was thinking *surely* I didn't place it in the donate pile. I could not find it. So I went to 'The Grab' hoping it would still be there. I walked in and *the very first thing* I laid my eyes on was her robe.

It was like I had found a treasure. I looked thru the other clothes and found more of her things. I had an armful. I didn't care how much it was going to cost me to buy her clothes back. I left with a bag *full* of her things, for $7. $7. I thought it was so ironic. $7 for a bag full of clothes and they were worth *so* much more to me.

Maybe we feel cast aside, ostracized, unloved, donated, worthless, useless. But what God does for us is he searches us out, seeks us, finds us. We are his treasure. The apple of his eye. God sent his son Jesus who paid the ultimate price for us—death on the cross. We are loved. Loved by the creator himself.

Thank you, *everyone*, for the happy birthday wishes and prayers. I appreciate them *all*. Very strange celebrating my first birthday since my mom went home to heaven three weeks ago, but she always celebrated me. She would say to me now, "Don't cry for me, I am perfect. Baby Girl, you are way braver than me. You go out there and do all the things that God has called you to do. Kiss my boys for me. I love you more." Psalm 34:18.

What do you do when emotion just punches you in your teeth? Out of the blue…like a sucker punch. You're just chipper, and smiling, and bringing your little bit of sunshine to the world…and *bam*! Somebody says something that triggers you. You smell a certain scent. You hear a certain song. What are you supposed to do? You were bringing the sunshine just a minute ago. But then, Barry says, "Button, button, who's got the button?" He doesn't know. That's the game that Ma played with the boys. So, what do you do? I tell you what you do. You go to the bathroom, sit on the throne, and sob and let the tears roll down your face. You super ugly cry and suck in air and hiccup and you *feel* it. The loss. The sadness. The anger. The pride (she was a great Ma). You ask God to please, please, please bless you with peace that passes all understanding. You feel. You cry. Then you leave that bathroom stall and wipe your face with cold paper towels. And you go back to work.

I wanted to cry during church—*all through church*. I wanted to cry. I was holding back tears, especially during worship. But I couldn't cry. I wore makeup today. So, I thought, *Later, I can cry later*. I can let it out later. Then we had a family event. No crying there. Then we had a banquet. Can't really cry there. After the banquet I had errands to focus on. So that's what I did, focused on my errands. Now, I'm home, sitting down and eating some dinner with my family. We're having good conversation and some laughs. For now, I don't want to cry. It feels good to not be on the verge of tears. For now, maybe, hopefully the urge to cry won't come tomorrow. But I can deal with that tomorrow. Tomorrow's a new day. But truthfully, today's not over.

It's been three months since my mom went to heaven. I still can't believe she's not here with us. I can't believe that she has been gone now for a longer time span than she was even sick. She has now been with Jesus longer even than from the day she broke her arm. That was the first indication that something was actually wrong, that something was going on in my mom's body and it wasn't good. I still look at my phone and see that I have a text message and I think it's from her. Still, things happen and I pick my phone up to text her to let her know what's going on, only to be smacked back to this new realty in which I realize I can't send text messages to heaven.

So after these three months, I'm still sad. I still want to cry. I still lose my composure at times. But I'm trying to find my happy. And it does show up at times, and actually it shows up a little more often than it did at first. That's the way my mom would want it. She wouldn't want any of us to be sad. She loved happy too much for us to stay so sad. I'm realizing that I need new encouragement. I always, always covet prayers. I appreciate warm hugs and sincere 'I love yous'. What I don't need are sad eyes. I'm sad enough as it is. So I'm asking, please don't bring your sad eyes to me. I need your bright eyes and a big heartfelt smile on your face. That would be encouraging. I also understand that you may be sad, too. I understand that possibly you still miss her as well. I understand that. But I really, really need your positivity. Please bring me your love, warm hugs, bright eyes, and shiny smiles. If you continue to bring me your sad eyes, I will avoid you. Not to be rude, it's just a type of defense mechanism. I have to defend myself from more sad if I can. I'm searching for my happy. If I want to see sad eyes I can look in the mirror. So please, honestly, please bring me your happy, bright eyes. That's what I need now.

I'm realizing more and more that ultimately, we have to go through our grief on our own. It's great and such a blessing to have wonderful family and friends that support you and pray for you. But when it comes to the alone times, the quiet times, the special times, the significant times…it really has to be just me and God. We have to be alone together and work through it, cry through it together. Sometimes there are special events that we must be alone to go through them. Go through them alone together, just you and God.

My tears aren't coming every single day anymore. It seems I've been saving them for shower time only. Oh…how I've been biting my lip to keep the tears at bay. But now, my tears are coming for my entire shower time, and then they want to continue after my shower time. Maybe biting my lip hasn't been working after all. When in the world do I have time to cry, and cry, and cry, and cry until I can't cry anymore. I literally don't have that kind of time. I have a job, and my people, and stuff. I have stuff. No time to cry.

And what if I have an allotted number of tears that I should release? If I hold them in for shower time, that's why they want to continue after I get out of the shower. What do I do now? Hope no one knocks on the bathroom door.

My husband and boys haven't seen me cry in a while. Maybe I should let them see me. See my grief that still smacks me in the face. Christmas is coming soon. Why can't my mom still be here with us? Why did God need her back home? We still need her here. Sometimes I try to think of all the times that she drove me crazy or got on my nerves, but very, very quickly I'm reminded of *all* of her selflessness. All the times she bailed me out. All the times she came in clutch for me. *All* the prayers she prayed for me and for my family.

So much love! She created the family she never had. She *prayed to have* the family she never had. I miss her *so* much. My phone 'dinged' alerting me I had a new text this evening and I literally thought, *That's probably Mom.* Nope. Not mom, texting from heaven. There is no love like a mother's love. No one has your back like your Momma. Nothing and no one can replace a mother's love for her child.

So, I keep going. I don't have any other choice. I keep praying for God to bless me. "The *Lord* is close to the brokenhearted and saves those who are crushed in spirit." I believe God's Word to be true. That's my only hope. Eternity. Death of the saints becomes eternal life in heaven with God through our Savior, Jesus the Christ.

Please excuse me. Excuse…attempt to lessen the blame attaching to (a fault or offense); seek to defend or justify. Excuse my standoffishness (if that's a word). Excuse me when I don't smile. Excuse me when I have to walk away. Please give me a pass. It's not you, it's me. Yes, I get up every day and go to work. I do my best to be the good wife, the good mother, the good daughter. There are moments I feel like being silly. There are moments I feel like laughing. There are more moments when I sit still and suddenly my eyes start leaking; sometimes, it's only a small leak, other times, the dam is broken, then my throat makes gasping and howling noises. These happen in private.

In my truck.

In my closet.

Me.

Alone.

The really happy times can also bring the sadness. It bubbles up like hot lava, forcing its burning self through tiny cracks in the happiness.

So yes, if you would, please excuse me.

Christmas is getting closer. At the beginning of the season I basically wanted to avoid as much "Christmas" as possible. Just skim through, just doing the basics. But as I've forced myself to listen to Christmas music, attend Christmas parades and Christmas programs, I can feel the joy, slowly but surely. And as the time is drawing near, my goodness, we have so much to be thankful and worshipful for. God sent his Son down to Earth as an infant to be our propitiation for sin. God has suffered loss, too.

So it goes…we "make it through" a certain holiday or event, only to be slapped in the face and brought to our knees with grief. I "made it through" Christmas Eve and Christmas Day, to then be wound tighter than a drum and angry. Frustrated. I "made it through" but what was my reward? Where was my prize? December 26 felt like someone dumped twenty-five dump truck loads of manure on me. Mad. That's what I was. Mad. Mad and angry. Angry that we had to do Christmas without my mom with us. Angry that I had to look into my dad's sad, brown eyes. Angry that all I had left of my mom was a blanket made from her clothes, and her mother's ring. I wanted my mom there. We all needed the glue of our Ma. So on December 26, I broke. Lost it again. When will this grief go away? I know my mom wouldn't want me being *so* sad. So I went for a drive. It was fast. But good. A sunny day. Cool wind in my hair. It felt really, really good. And I listened to worship music. And after a while, I knew (again), that everything was gonna be okay. I never realized that these holidays and family events were going to be *so very hard*. I've suffered loss before, but not like this. So I took my drive and worshiped and arrived home with a renewed spirit. I hope the sun is shining tomorrow.

Again no sunshine. I'm beginning to question my choice for living destinations. I definitely need more sunshine. Also, I had a doctor visit today. Not a regular check-up, a specialty visit. Nothing special, but also not routine. Anyway...the question was asked regarding why I've not been running as much recently as I had been running in the past. Partly because my legs are tired after work and my legs are heavy, but mostly...because I'm sad. This physician then asked me if I had spoken to my primary care physician about taking "medication for mood stabilization." What? Umm...no. It's called grief. I'm managing. I'm working through it.

We have all these "firsts" that we have to "make it through." I'm not a pill person. That's perfectly fine if you have an actual hormonal imbalance and you need a pill to help you stabilize and function. It's okay. But for me, I don't want to rely on a pill to hopefully get me through. I just need to grieve. It's a process. I'm sad. For me, it doesn't require a pill. I need to grieve my loss and I need to rely on my God to get me through. Yes, I'll be sad. But as of today, I'm going to try so hard to not be sad, but to be grateful instead. Not to mourn my loss, but to rejoice in my future and in my eternity. I need to change my thought process. Instead of being sad that my mom's not here, I want to be rejoicing that I had such a great mom, and that she is in heaven worshiping King Jesus.

Well, no sunshine today. Just gray clouds…and rain… Not to mention that I have to hear about other people and their mother's fight/battle with cancer. I want to say, "Can you please shut up! Are you so selfish that you want to talk about your mom and her struggle with cancer and have you forgotten that my mom is gone? She's gone from here! My mom is gone! Please quit talking about your mom."

But then another part if me wants to say, "Cherish this time with your mother. Care for her. Help her. Ask her questions. Ask her the hard questions. Ask her what she would do differently. Ask her where her living will is and make sure you sign paperwork for power of attorney. Ask her the passwords for her online accounts. Ask her if there are any letters that she would like to write to people. Make sure her Last Will and Testament are in order. Show your mom love and have honest conversations." That's what I want to say.

But…I say *nothing*. Just nothing. I don't want to stir the pot or rock the boat either way. Besides, if I verbally, out loud, said anything at all, I would lose my composure and be stuck in the bathroom to collect myself. So I'll just be quiet. Not one word. No questions asked. No words spoken. No advice shared. Quiet.

"Though the mountains may crumble, you will not." It's been almost four months since mom left for home. I miss her a lot. Getting through Christmas and the New Year was a struggle, I can't lie. But in the past week I've come to realize that I *must* change my mindset and my thought process. I cannot dwell on how much I miss my mom and how much I really, really wish she was still here with us. I have to focus instead on the incredible memories I have and laugh at the crazy stuff she did. The eight weeks that she was so sick and deteriorating every single day were such a muddled time. Trying to stay positive and uplifting, trying to be helpful and be encouraging; then leaving broken to bits with my soul shattered. I grieved inwardly and pretended outwardly. Those days were hard. More than hard. They were excruciating in so many ways. Praying for a miracle but knowing what God had spoken to me. So I think about that time often, but I realize I cannot dwell there, I must dig deeper. My roots have to push through to find nutrients. I have fresh fruit to produce for my next season. God will take my crushed spirit, and when I lean into him, he will take my pain and make me stronger for his plan and his purpose.

I can feel my spirit shifting. My joy is returning. My husband and I had a couple of days of downtime together with plenty of unrushed hours and no distractions. We had some hard conversations and quiet walks in the woods together. Conversations with your very best friend can be so relieving and revealing; like a weight has been lifted from your shoulders. Your yoke is lighter. Your yoke is shared. Sharing your deepest feelings and thoughts can be like a breath of fresh air. Remember when you were a kid and swimming with your friends, competing to see who could hold their breath underwater for the longest time, when you thought your lungs would explode and your eyes might actually pop out of your head, you push to the surface and gasp the air to fill your lungs and it's such a relief. It's kind of strange, that feeling of your lungs about to explode, it's not because they are full of good air but because they need fresh air. Sometimes we feel the same. We're about to explode. We have to share our feelings and have hard conversations in order to be filled with fresh air. As my joy is returning and the sadness leaks from my eyes less often, I have a genuine smile on my face and a song in my heart. I feel a pep in my step and I want to dance a little more. Joy feels nice. I am thankful.

Five months. The twelfth of the month, and Valentine's Day to follow. I knew it would be difficult, and difficult for my dad as well. So, I pushed head long. I baked and made the Valentine cookies that my Momma always made. My boys were in the kitchen helping me roll the cookie dough while Dewayne was cooking dinner. (I've always said the real action happens in the kitchen. Lol!)

Anyway, it was a sweet time, sweeter even than the cookies. I was sad for a moment but I've learned that I can't dwell on the sadness. I have to be sad for a moment and feel all my feelings and then I have to change my mindset. There have been *so* many instances in the last few days where I have literally turned around to reach for my phone to text my mom to see what she's doing, then realization hits and I remember she's in heaven and I can't text her, but I know she's perfect. I've needed to ask her some questions recently and I've needed her advice. So I just have to take some quiet moments and think about what she would tell me. The answers have come. God knew I wasn't strong enough to make it in this world without my mom, but he is strong enough. He is my strength. My strength comes from the Lord.

You can't live in the darkness and expect to feel like you're living in the light.

Yesterday I was online shopping for headbands. I was looking for a gift for my friend's birthday. While scrolling through all of the beautifully colored and designed headbands, I came upon different head wraps, the kind you typically wear after losing hair from chemotherapy. One glance at those and I became physically nauseated. It was instant. During my mom's chemotherapy treatments (of which she only received two), she had begun to lose her hair and started wearing a scarf. She quickly decided to shave off all of her hair because the slow loss of it was frustrating. Her hair was getting in her mouth and in her eyes and was piling up in her chair. So, she got rid of it. After my sister-in-law shaved her head, she took a picture of my mom and sent it to me. That was the last photo taken of my mom and the biggest smile on her face that I had seen in a while. Seeing the picture made me both happy, and extremely sad. Mom only wore those head coverings a handful of times after that. I didn't come to hate them until after she passed. I actually had forgotten about the head coverings until I scrolled upon them.

It's true what they say about grief sneaking up on you, out of the blue, catching you off guard. It's a real thing. So I just took a moment and felt the hurt, anger, disappointment, and sadness. I tried to remember the head coverings that she had worn. I thought for a moment about all the pain that she had been experiencing, the constant nausea she dealt with, how her mobility had become almost zero, and she still lived with a broken dominant right arm that couldn't be fixed. Then I remembered where she is, on streets of gold, walking with Jesus without pain and totally healed and made new. I acknowledged my nausea; then I scrolled on.

Well...I almost made it through the twelfth day of the month without breaking down...almost. Somehow I had the day off work. It was a gift. A special day off after being on call. A rare treat. A treasure. So I spent the morning enjoying my coffee, and devotionals, and prayer time. My coffee with Jesus. Unrushed. Peaceful. The sun was shining. A beautiful day. I went for a drive with the sunroof open and my music blasting. Had a nice lunch by myself. No thirty-minute unpaid time limit. Just me enjoying my Five Guys. Had a couple of errands that went well, then drove home. The open road. At home I enjoyed a few minutes on the front porch in my rocking chair, my granny's rocker, watching the sun float down slowly into the setting. I even received an invitation from Isaac, "Hey Mom, come here. Let me ball up on you." The cu da gra of invitations, to play backyard basketball with my boy. So we balled for a bit. Of course I mostly was dramatic and laughed like a hyena mixed with some screaming, but that's just what I do. We came in and had dinner together, the four of us. Then Isaac went to being his namesake. Isaac, "he who laughs" or "laughter." He was being so silly and dancing in the hallway, a thousand percent entertaining us. Laughing out loud! Then my dad called me. One of Isaac's sweet friends had taken my daddy some food and my dad was looking for advice on whether or not he should call that person to thank them again for thinking of him. We had a little conversation and chatted a minute. When I hung up, I just couldn't hold my tears in, they spilled out before I could even catch my breath.

Six months ago Mom went to live in heaven. I said to Dewayne and Treven, "Today is six months you know. I don't know if the twelfth of the month will ever pass by without me noticing." So, I had to cry. A beautiful, sunny day spent driving, and singing, and laughing ended in tears. It's not what I had planned. But I don't think it's what we ever have planned. You know, "A man's heart plans his way, but the Lord directs his steps" (Proverbs 16:9). We have to accept whatever comes our way. Joy and tears, happiness and sorrow, sunshine and rain. Right now I'm so thankful that when I do leave this Earth, I know I will spend eternity in heaven. Thank you, Jesus. "Weeping may endure for the night but joy comes in the morning" (Psalm 30:5b).

Seven months now since Mom passed away. It's unbelievable still. I think about her every single day, multiple times a day actually. The past month has been a good one; the sun has been out more with much less rain and the gray skies have largely departed. The grass is becoming green and flowers are starting to bloom.

The past couple of weeks I have been more sad. Treven's track season has started and I know that my Mom would love, love, love watching him run so beautifully. Isaac's birthday is coming up shortly (this is another story for later) and Easter is just around the corner. All of these events make me miss her more, which may be why I dreamed about my mom yesterday for the very first time since her passing.

Daddy has dreamed about her and she has showed up in my brother's dreams. I wondered, why not me? But anyway, I had an opportunity to take a nap yesterday. I'm a huge fan of naps. I'm fairly certain there is something in my DNA to prove my need for them. But during my short nap is when my mom appeared in my dream. When she popped in, of course she was being bossy and passing along some 'helpful and necessary information' to me. At first I was irritated with her, but then it was like my dream turned to reality and I realized my mom had appeared in front of me. I ran over to her and hugged her tight. Tears began to flow down my cheeks. I woke myself up sobbing with tears dripping onto my pillow. I wanted so bad to go back to my dream. Maybe Mom had something to tell me. We could spend a little time together in my dream. But, no I was awake now.

I lay there for a moment realizing it was actually a dream; everything had been so vivid I wasn't convinced. Then a smile came across my face. What a sweet time I had just experienced! Having this dream made me realize Mom is with me at track meets, she'll be there for Isaac's birthday, and she surely wouldn't miss Easter with us. Obviously I am aware that she isn't physically here and she is in heaven with our Savior, Jesus Christ, who was crucified on the cross and rose from the grave three days later. I can't even begin to imagine her Easter celebration each and every day with Jesus.

Eight months today since mom went home, and today happens to be Mother's Day as well. The past couple of weeks have been pretty difficult, seeing all of the Mother's Day gifts displayed, and all of the ads and commercials for Mother's Day. Several times I've seen some potted flowers or hanging baskets, kitchen towels, coffee cups, or jewelry, and thought, *Oh Mom would love that*, or *I would usually be buying something like that, but not this year.*

I never knew Mother's Day could be so sad or would ever be so sad for me. Of course I'm thrilled beyond words to be a mom myself and have two sons, and I have so much joy in my life because of them, so Mother's Day isn't altogether overwhelmingly sad. I'm very thankful and grateful. I've had to pray a little bit extra lately, just for God to please send me his peace and grace, to fill the hole and the ache in my heart when I just miss my mom so much and I just wish she was here.

Lately I've tried focusing more on how great my mom was and all that she meant to me. I've listened to some of her voicemails that I had saved on my phone. I've been reflecting on so many things that she did for me throughout my entire life and how much she loved me and her grandchildren. It's still hard when I see an older woman with her mother. I think I had always looked forward to the day when my mom and I could spend more time together after my husband and I became empty nesters. A time when we would all be in different and new phases in our lives. My mom was so blessed to spend so much time with her mother after all the grands had started school. They had lunch often and took short day trips to visit other family members. I looked forward to the day that my mom and I would be able to do the same. But God's plans are not our plans and he saw fit to take my mom home. Still I know that God loves us and his plans for us are good.

We live in a fallen world with sin and death, pain and heartbreak, but our joy comes from the Lord. And we must choose joy.

It seems like it has been the longest month, yet time seems to be passing so quickly. All I know right now is that one day I hope I wake up and it's the fourteenth or fifteenth of the month and I have an 'ah ha' moment that the twelfth has passed and I didn't even know it. I begin to realize that the twelfth is coming. I'm not sure when, what day specifically, it just becomes a realization. And I dread it. I seriously can't believe that my mom has been gone now for (almost) nine months. Enough time for a baby to be made, grow, develop, and be born. That's the entire amount of time that my mom has been in heaven. I don't know exactly what would have become of me up to this point if I didn't do my daily scripture reading and Bible study, along with my prayer time every morning. I've also been challenging myself physically at the gym every single day. I decided that I had been emotionally and mentally challenged, so why not pour in a physical challenge too? I've loved it. God, prayer, the Bible (scripture), the Holy Spirit, worship, and challenging myself physically have gotten me this far. And I've accomplished things I never imagined. So, I'm gonna keep pushing. Keep praising the Lord. Being open to opportunities to serve Him. Seeking daily, hour by hour, minute by minute, guidance from the Holy Spirit. My mom would be proud.

Ephesians 3:20.

July 12 arrived and passed. I was much less focused on the fact that my Mom has been away from us and in heaven for ten months, and that it was exactly one year ago that she received her devastating diagnosis, but I was instead hyper aware that July 12 was her birthday. That's pretty much all I could think about. I was wishing I could call her and tell her happy birthday. Wishing I could send her a text message and some flowers. Missing the fact that I couldn't have her over for dinner Friday or Saturday night. I had contemplated taking the day off work but decided against it. I'm glad I went to work instead. We had a busy day and I didn't have time to stop and ponder.

That afternoon, my dad accompanied me and my husband to a football seven on seven that our youngest son was playing in. We had a quiet ride with the a/c blowing. (My mom wouldn't have come with us because it was super hot and humid, and she wouldn't want to sit out in the heat; and my dad wouldn't have come because he would have stayed home with my mom.) But times are different and Pa gets out a little more than Ma did in that regard. But the three of us enjoyed our football watching (football is my happy place), then we had a quiet ride back home with the windows down and the cooler mountain air blowing around us, while appreciating the stunning sunset that God gifted us that evening. We didn't speak of Ma, I know it's because we each knew that she had been constantly on our minds all day individually. I know there has not been a single day that has passed that I haven't thought about her multiple times. My phone will alert that I have received a text message and I still think, *Oh, it's probably Mom.*

I do wish God would give me more "signs" of my mom. There was a beautiful orange and black butterfly in the garage with me two weeks ago. It just lighted on the ladder and lingered there for hours. I would leave to go do other chores and come back and the butterfly was still there. I did feel like it was a sign from God. He knew I was needing that because of some stress I had been experiencing. I do wish I had more of those instances, but I do sense my mom when my wind chimes hit a single note, and I sometimes can feel my mom in the breeze. So, God is getting us through day by day. It's different. Our new normal. But we are making it.

Somehow, it's seems like forever since I last wrote. But it's literally been a month. If you asked me if I thought July passed quickly, I would definitely, resoundingly, emphatically reply "*Yes!*" But still it seems like it's been so long since I've written. So, anyway, we've arrived at eleven months since my mom went to our heavenly home. It's still so, so strange to say my mom isn't here with us any longer. Sometimes it still doesn't seem real, like just something that exists in an alternate universe. That sounds super weird I know. I guess I'm just saying that it's my reality, but it still doesn't seem real.

I just competed in a bodybuilding competition a week ago and the twenty weeks of training was excellent therapy for me. It was life changing. Truly. The focus, dedication, and discipline that I poured into my training was an incredible journey for me. I'm not constantly sad. I was constantly sad before. Months ago, I was only having tiny glimpses of joy and I knew I needed to challenge myself. So I did. I posted my story on my Facebook and Instagram, so I won't repeat it here. But I'm changed because I determined to step outside of my comfort zone and challenge myself. I'm glad I did.

Today, I still miss my mom so much. But I have so much more joy in my life. God helped me move myself into a different space. Often times recently, I just really miss my mom being here to share in *all* of the *great* things that my boys are doing. Isaac is a three-star rated high school football player and received an invitation to play in the Blue-Grey All-American Bowl in Dallas, Tx, in December. *Yikes!* That's so incredible and my mom would be beyond excited! And Treven is doing a phenomenal job on the football field and is literally improving every time he steps on the field. His coaches have shared some jaw-dropping information with us, and my mom would be so very proud. She loved all of her grands so much!

So, often times recently, I just super miss her being here to share in the excitement of all the spectacular news that we've been given. And I'm trying to learn how to deal with all of that; receiving wonderful information and then also processing the fact that my mom isn't here to share in the joy and excitement with us. But every day is easier. Not easy, but easier. The overwhelming sadness is lifting. I no longer feel like I'm trying to function in daily life while also being covered with a weighted blanket. Some days felt like I had a weighted blanket on my chest while I'm trying to walk thru a mud pit up to my knees. That's the best way I can describe how I felt. But everything is changing. My joy for living is returning. And I'm happy. Again.

I can't believe it's been one year since my sweet mom got her angel wings. I still don't have adequate words to express how much I miss her and how she is so constantly on my mind and in my thoughts.

Two things I know for certain…she loved her family, and she prayed for all of us without ceasing.

I know that God brought us through this year, and His comfort has been palpable to me.

2 Corinthians 1:3–4

And I must honestly say that I was looking forward to writing today, but I have *so* many feelings and emotions, thoughts running through my head so quickly, I can't get everything out of my brain fast enough. I can't write today. I'm going to have to jot down all my thoughts and write them out later. It's all coming too fast today.

So, it's weird, but I'm still not ready to write again. Right now, I'm *still* learning that I need to let myself have my "moments" when they come because when I stifle my emotions, they erupt at slightly inappropriate times. I'm still dealing with the fact that my dad's helper is gone and I wish she was still here to help him. Constantly my heart breaks for him. And that makes me sad on top of the sadness I already have. He still talks to me about going through what is left of my mom's clothes, and I'm thinking we have been through everything; surely I don't have to go through that again. And, my dad had my mom's headstone placed at the grave the other day. I haven't been there yet. I'm not ready.

And still yet, since my mom donated her body to medical research (which I am very, very proud of by the way), we still haven't received my mom's cremains…so we still have yet to bury her ashes. I truly feel like I have closure up to now, but when we have to go pick up the cremains and bury them, I think everything will be completely raw for me, like a scab ripped off of a wound. Painful. Tender. I'm not exactly looking forward to that.

It's still so hard for me to know that my mom isn't here anymore. Like I totally am aware that I haven't talked to her since September 12, 2018. Believe me…I know this. And I completely know that I haven't texted her or bought her any gifts. I know she hasn't texted me to ask about the boys and how their week has been or how work is going for me. I know this. All too well. Yet, it still is surreal for me. Like some alternative universe. So alien and foreign. I'm still managing, struggling, begging God to be with me and guide me and send me peace and comfort. Most days are better than the day before. Some days are several steps back. It's a work in progress for certain. I know I wouldn't be where I am without my God and my Savior. My hope and strength.

It's November 17. I'm not sure how it's past the middle of November already. The twelfth came and went, thankfully. We have been busy with the boys, especially Isaac right now. So much stuff going on that my mom would be so proud. I do certainly still miss her text messages. I'm slowly realizing that she was literally the only person that texted me. Lol! I see Dewayne in the mornings and we text each other in the afternoons, but mom was the only person that checked on me every day because we didn't see each other every single day.

Anyway…I did finally make it to the cemetery this morning. An absolutely beautiful, sunny, crisp fall day. It's fifty-one degrees with a cool breeze blowing the leaves across the ground, wispy clouds, and jet contrails decorate the sky. It's peaceful here, just a field of cows across the barbwire fence and the hum of distant traffic occasionally. The headstone is pretty. My dad did a good job picking it out. So I've made the first step in getting out here to see it. I completely know that we'll be back to bury my mom's ashes in a few months. Good grief…I feel like this process is never ending. I know I'll always deal with the grief and the loss. I just honestly really hate cemeteries. No one is there. To me it's a place of the reminder of death. I don't need to be reminded. I feel like it's a spot that is left for your family to have to take care of. I had liked mom's first choice better, which was to have her ashes spread. But I know she ended up changing her mind shortly after her diagnosis and she wanted to be buried next to her mother because grandma is buried by herself. I guess mom didn't want grandma to be alone.

Anyway…I know I won't be out to the cemetery to visit to feel closer to my mom and that's just my own personal belief. Instead, I do feel closer to her when I wrap up in one of the blankets that I had made out of her clothes, or when I wear a special piece of her jewelry, or when I make special food that she used to make. But I do feel like seeing the headstone was a hurdle that I had to jump. Another part of the process that I had to conquer.

Maybe it's because Christmas will be here soon, but I've been super aware of the date. It's the twelfth of the month and Ma has been away for fifteen months. That's unbelievable. It's just unbelievable to me. She is on my mind every day, multiple times a day. Even this morning I was thinking about a trip we are leaving for tomorrow and I thought, *Oh...I'll have to send Ma lots of pictures. She'll want lots of pictures and frequent updates.* I wonder if the day will come when I don't have those immediate thoughts? I'm kind of guessing no; that day will never come. I honestly think that as old as I get, I will always have that immediate inclination to text my mom, or call my mom, or tell my mom, go see my mom, talk to my mom. And that's kind of the thing, in my mind, she will never be older than seventy. She will always be younger in my mind. So, it's always my chipper, joyful, helpful mom that is on my mind; the mom who was always willing to help me and was always there; the mom who always wanted to know what we were doing and how things were going and wanted me to send tons of pictures when we went out of town for trips.

So I guess that's just the thing. We were close and she's not someone that can fall out of my memory or daily thoughts in just a few months' time. It's just that those immediate thoughts to include her are constant reminders that she's still not here. I know I will always miss her advice and her wisdom. The person that loved me the most on the whole face of the Earth, and only and always wanted the very best for me. I could talk to her and get her point of view, and above everything else, I knew without a shadow of a doubt that she was praying for me. But it's okay. She gets to be in heaven celebrating Jesus on his birthday! Wow! That will be beyond amazing. God, I thank you for sending Jesus, that through him we have the opportunity to spend eternity in heaven with you.

I believe God speaks to me in sunsets. When he opens up the heavens at exactly the time that I am super stressed, he grabs my attention. Like a parent holds their child's jaw in their hand and looks them directly in the eyes; that's what God does to me when the clouds part and the sunset's rays burst forth with their radiance. That's when God says, "Hey, I have something I need to tell you, pay attention, let's talk for a minute."

I probably made the most awkward phone call of my life today. My brother has been in contact with the medical school where my mom wanted her body donated; he was our family liaison in all of that process. As the time is drawing closer for us to be able to pick up mom's cremains, I have been wanting more information so I can plan around my job in order to pick them up.

My brother has been very busy lately, so I made the phone call today. I spoke with a lovely lady. She is new at her job but she was very helpful. During our conversation, I implied that the pick-up date for my mom's cremains should be coming up very shortly. She informed me that my mom's body has very recently been in a class-room and used for instruction. I admit I was a bit shocked only because I thought the time was nearing the end and she would be released to us. After my initial shock wore off, I was emotional but immediately very proud. My mom is making a difference even after death. Super selfless if you ask me. Then the nice lady began giving me some instructions on how the ashes could be transferred and the paperwork that would be necessary. One of the options was to leave the ashes there and the medical school would have them buried in a cemetery that is on campus or near campus. Another option was to have the ashes mailed to us. I was shocked at this also and taken back a bit. I'm not intending to belittle anyone that may be in this posi-tion and would make that choice. Honestly, my brother might make this choice. And that's okay. We all have choices in life and we make the best choices for us based on our culture, conscience, and heart.

But I digress…anyway, the phone call ended with this kind lady promising to call me back within the next couple of days with the information of when my mom's ashes would be released. She said she would mail the proper paperwork to my dad so he could sign as next of kin for me to pick up mom's ashes. I still haven't talked with my dad about whether he wants to ride six hours with me to pick them up or if it's okay if I just show up at his house with them. Right now I'm guessing the latter. He's not much on road trips, especially long trips with a two-hour turn around. So, at least I made it through this strange phone call, and soon I'll have more information on when I can pick up the ashes and we can finish the process with burying them at the cemetery where my mom's headstone awaits.

I got the phone call this afternoon that my mom's ashes are ready to be picked up. How do I tell my dad this information? I have to give him a heads up that the paperwork will be arriving on Saturday or Monday in the mail and the papers need to be signed and mailed back. I know I'll have to work late tomorrow night and I'm on call Saturday and Sunday. Do I tell him with other people around? Do I tell him at church Sunday morning in the hopes that the paperwork didn't arrive in the mail on Saturday? My dad won't break down in front of me. It'll be when he's alone. I do believe he would break down in front of my brother, but not me. My brother and I have totally different views on how well my dad is coping. I think it's because he relates to both of us differently. Anyway, I'm gonna pray about it and see what God says to me.

So…I went over to my dad's this evening and told him everything. He did well. His voice cracked a little and his eyes got moist but he did okay. God is our only hope and strength. He gives us hope to keep going and enduring this process.

Daddy called. He received the paperwork in the mail today to fill out so we can pick up Mom's ashes. He of course wants me and my brother to help him fill it out because he doesn't want to do anything wrong. I promise, the healing scab is ripped off with every single event. I don't want to deter anyone/someone from donating their body to science and research. I'm proud of my mom for making that decision, especially considering her health history, but just know that the grief process begins anew. It's like lava that bubbles up and erupts from the mountaintop and slowly flows down the side of the mountain. It burns all over again. But I know diamonds are created under pressure, over time and are spewed out from the deep layers of Earth in the lava. It will burn, but the sparkle is there.

My dad and I drove five hours one-way to pick up my mom's ashes this past Tuesday. We left early in the morning. It was cloudy but not raining. The sun broke through the clouds as we drove, brightening the day a bit. When we arrived in Memphis, we drove past Sun Records Recording Studio, The Peabody Hotel, then down to see the Mississippi River. Then we circled back to campus and met with the very kind man that is the director of anatomical donations. The building where we met, walked in then took the elevator, was kind of cold, plain, and a bit sterile. But he was very gracious and kind, thanking us several times for allowing them to have my mom's donation. Then dad and I left with mom's ashes in a box in the back seat.

We drove down Beale Street and ate Memphis BBQ at Blues City Cafe. (This trip was the first time my dad had ever been to Memphis and this was actually the furthest West my dad had ever been). The sun was shining bright and was warm through the windows of the cafe. We enjoyed our lunch together. Then we left and drove five hours back home. We had a nice trip.

Oddly, somehow, I felt like mom was back with us. I know she's been in heaven for sixteen months now, but just having her ashes with us, in our possession, made me feel at peace; like she was back with our family where she belongs. The sunset behind me told the story of my future. Not a sunset that was soft and scattered through clouds, but a big, bright, flaming ball of fire; my future is hopeful, and is going to be exciting, fun, an adventure and risky all at the same time. I dropped dad at home and brought mom's ashes home with me. She needed to spend more time at my new house anyway.

What a great weekend. Speaking of high highs and low lows...this was it. Friday night, Isaac received an email that he was accepted to the University of Tennessee for Fall admission. *What a smile on that kid's face!*. We (me, Dewayne, and Treven) had a turn up in the boys' bathroom while Isaac was in the shower. LOL! Proud mom here!

Saturday, Treven was an absolute stunner in his tuxedo as an usher at the Sweetheart Pageant. Breaking my heart and making my heart swell at the same time.

Then Sunday, we buried my mom's ashes. I so do not want to linger here. I want so much to keep focusing on my happy place and the future; like my oldest son being accepted to UT Knoxville, and my youngest son being a smoke show. My mom would be *so* proud... like beyond herself proud. I miss her, and I miss that she is missing our lives. How do I keep carrying on without my mom? How have I continued to carry on the past sixteen months without her? I don't carry on. My God carries me.

On February 2, we buried my mom's ashes. It was a beautiful, sunny Sunday. A beautiful blue sky, no clouds to be seen. The temperature was even a little bit on the warm side, but a cool breeze was blowing. My sweet dad and my uncle (his brother) had gone out two days before to dig the hole where we would place the ashes. Our family gathered around the gravesite and my brother placed the ashes in the ground and shoveled the dirt on top. I placed the arrangement of roses on top of the grass. As I leaned over to place the roses, it was all I could do to not drop to my knees and weep. I really wanted to. I wanted to throw the roses down and then fall to my knees and release all the sobs that I had been choking back. But instead, I stood back up. I gathered my family. I asked everyone to come closer. I wanted to pray. The men always pray. Always my husband or my brother. But I needed to pray. I needed to pray at my mom's grave. I needed to gather my family and pray.

During this entire process of my mom's Stage 4 cancer diagnosis, her health declining, my dad providing her care every single day, me caring for my mom in her very last days, her death when my dad, brother, and I were with her, and the darkness, sadness, and struggle since, I've realized so many things. One of those realizations has been that we all grieve differently. Another thing I've realized has been that different people mean different things to us. I was close to my mom and her death has been extremely difficult for me. Another person may not be as close to their mom, so their grief and loss will look far different from mine. So I've come to know that the loss of my mother to me may look quite different from someone else's loss of their mother. This applies to all other family members and friends. And that makes our grief different. That makes our grieving processes very different.

Someone said to me, "it doesn't get any better," referring to the grief and heartbreak that I was experiencing the day we buried my mom's ashes. I miss my mom every single day. I think about my mom every single day. My mom was part of me. She was a part of my daily life. Honestly, there are times when I just shake my head because I honestly can't believe she is actually not physically here anymore. My sweet mom is not here. Then I remind myself of God's truths. All the scripture that I have stored up in my heart and mind. And I *know* that it does get better. Yes, there are days that I want to cry. Yes, there are days when I don't want to get out of bed. Yes, there are still days that I come home from work and I can't make myself do anything else but lay on the couch. But those days are rare. I can tell you that it does get better. My joy has returned.

God has given me new purpose. Out of the dust, the potter molds new vessels. Some days are fine and other days are worse. But my God loves me and cares for me and his plans are good. He is our hope and he has a purpose for us. You only have to believe and have faith. And in all of this, I believe that when I pass from this earthly life, I will spend eternity in heaven with my mom and with my heavenly Father. I pray the rest of my family will be there too, gathered together forever.

About the Author

Shannon is a Jesus worshiper, wife, mother, daughter, nurse, friend, and newly published author. Born and raised in the hills of East Tennessee, Shannon enjoys spending time with her family, reading, weight training, everything about football, beach vacations, all things summer, and a good adventure.